Vander Cook Etudes

by H. A. Vander Cook

Published for:

*CORNET or TRUMPET

(Baritone Treble Clef — Eb Alto — Mellophone)

● *TROMBONE or BARITONE (Bass Clef)

(Transcribed and Edited by Walter C. Welke)

Eb or BBb BASS (Tuba)

* Bb Cornet, Trumpet, Trombone, and Baritone are playable together.

RUBANK®

HAL•LEONARD®
CORPORATION
7777 W BLUEMOUND RD PO BOX 13819 MILWAUKEE, WI 53213

VanderCook Etudes for Trombone or Baritone

Transcribed and Edited by
WALTER C. WELKE

* Numbers refer to Trombone positions throughout. Parentheses indicate optional positions: (5).

*( ) = optional.

6

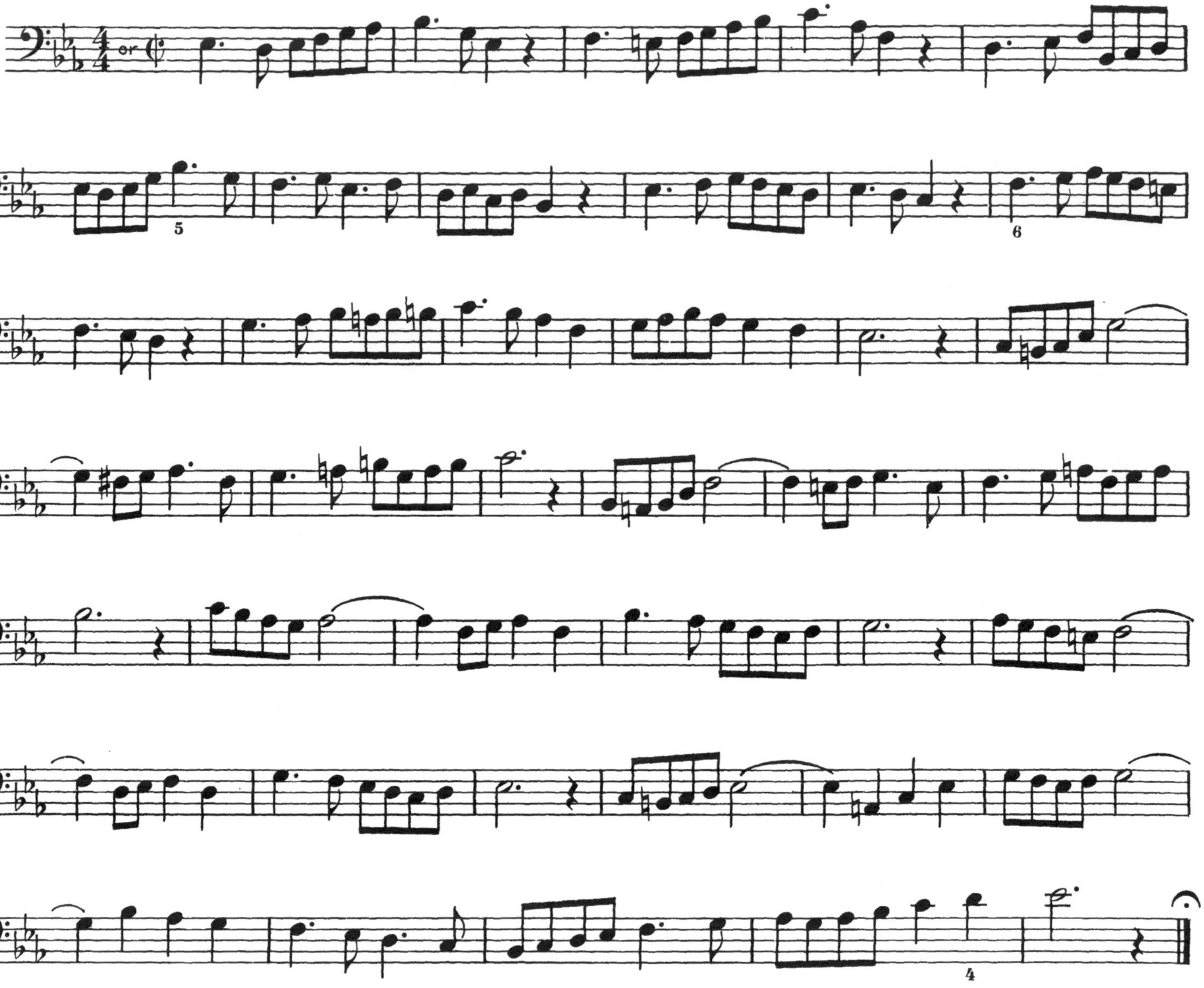

7

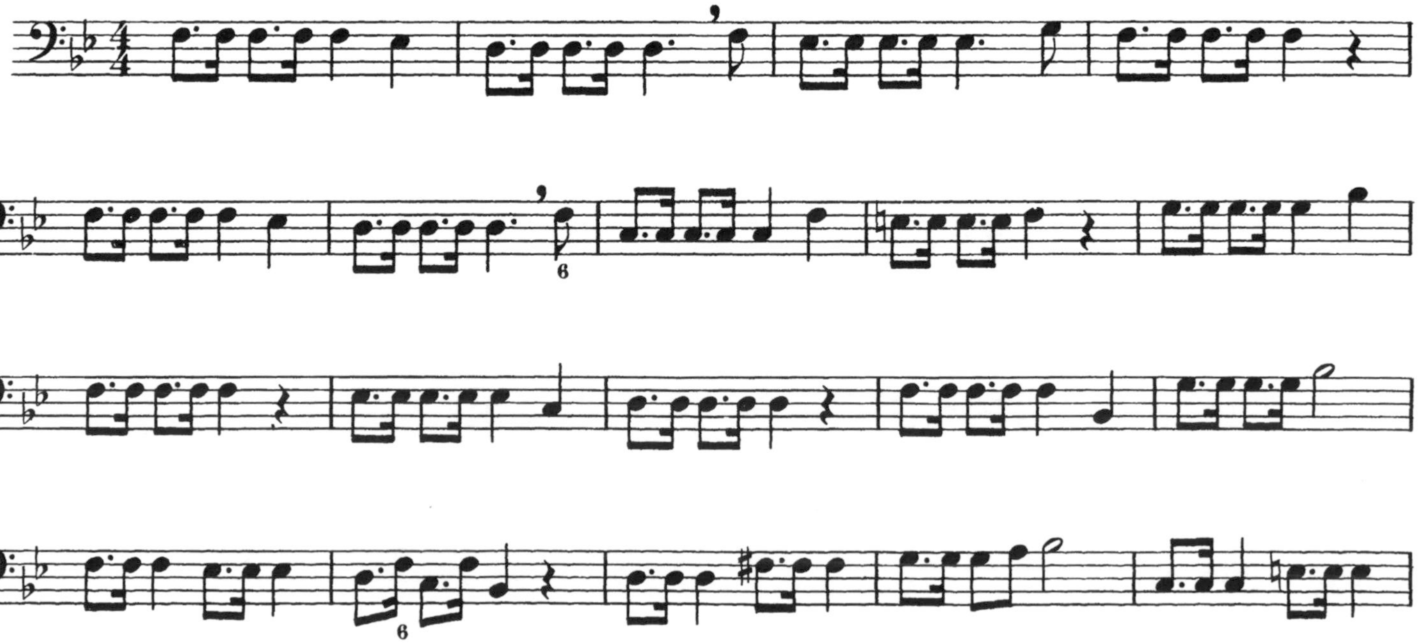

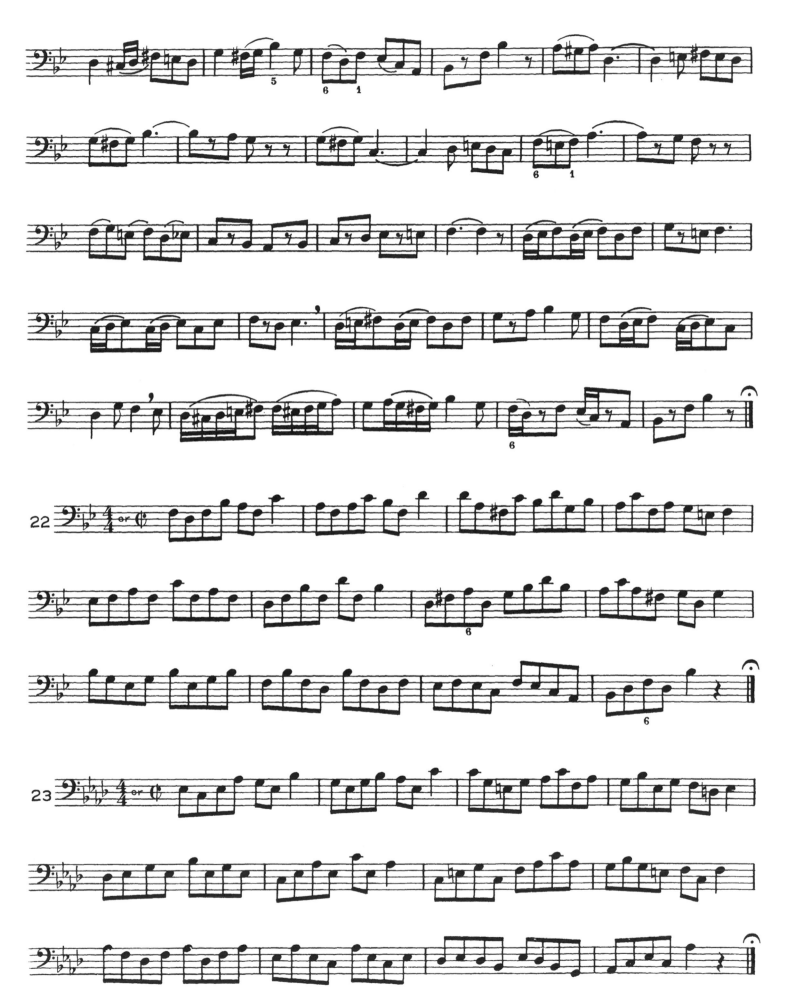

28
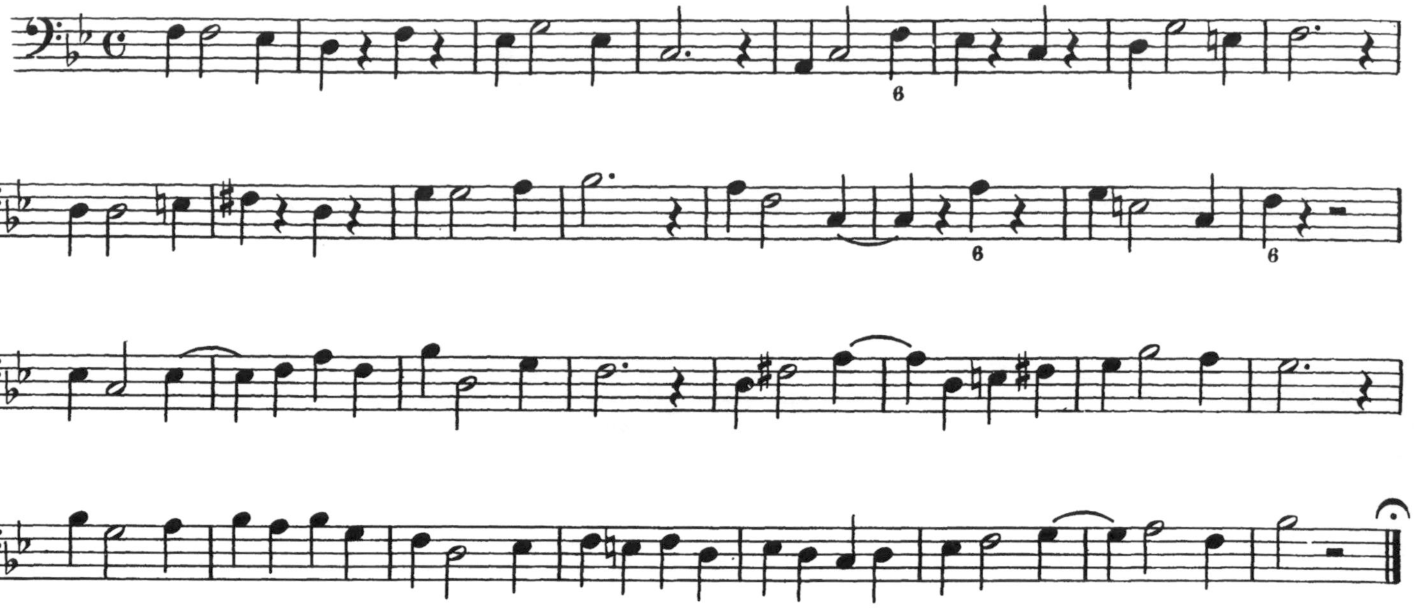

29
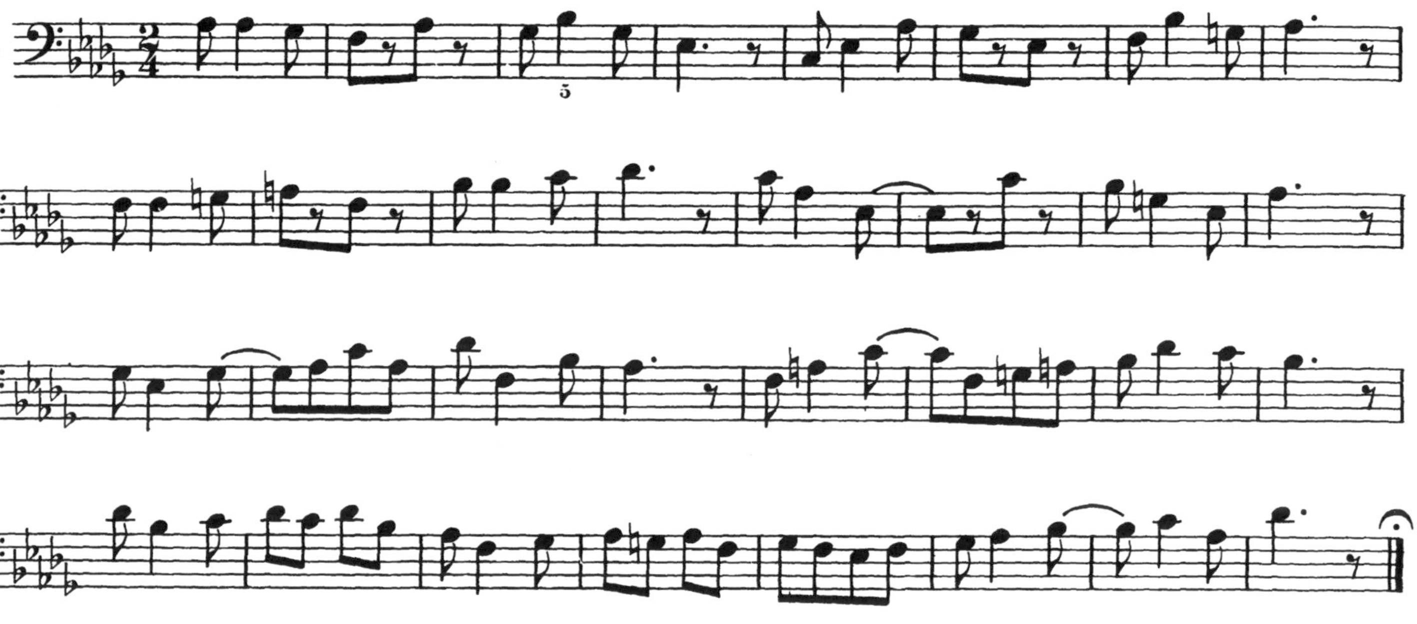

30
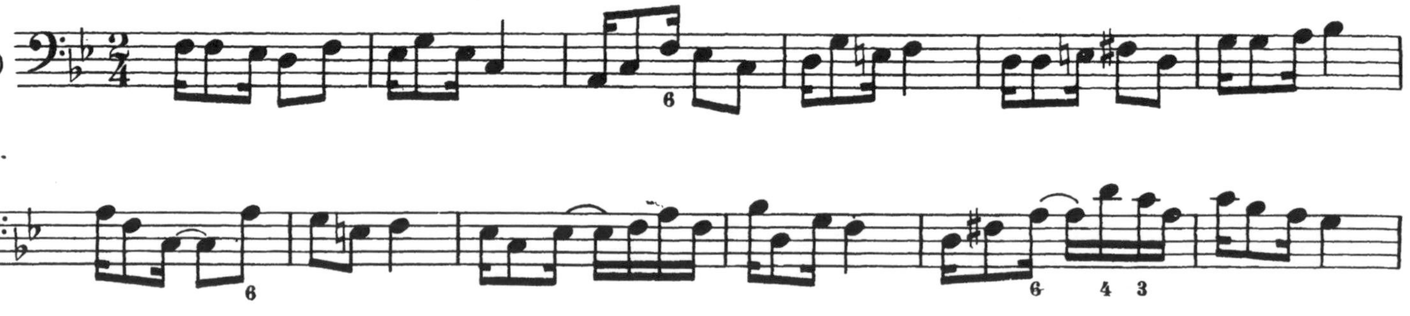

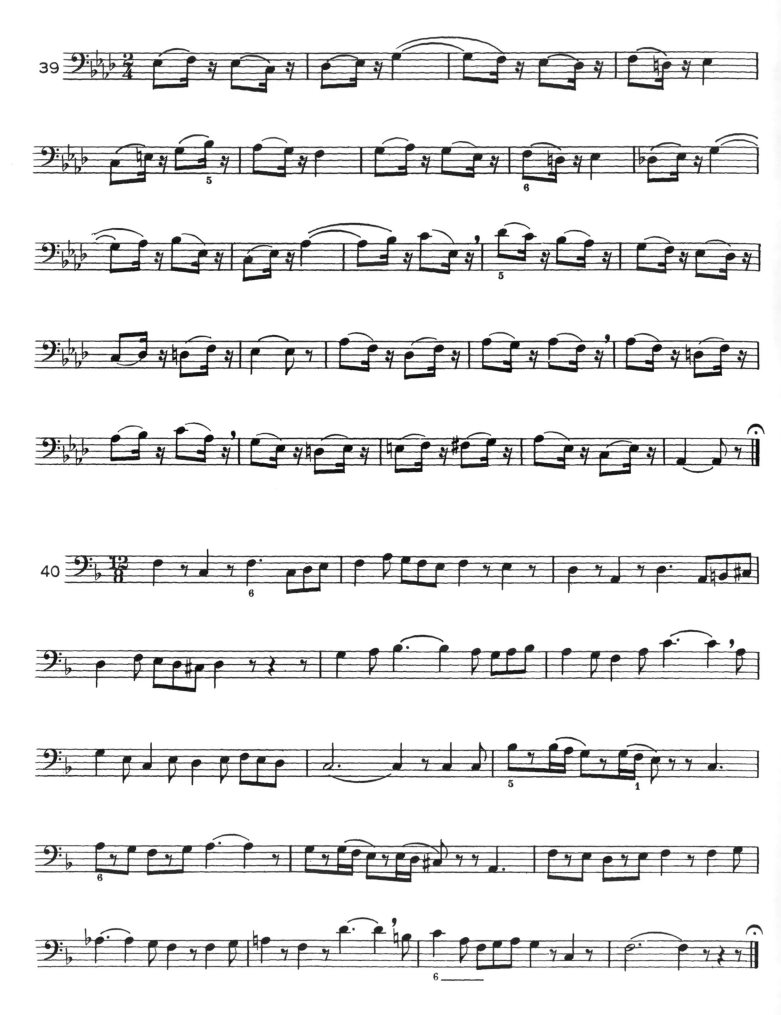

Waltz tempo

47

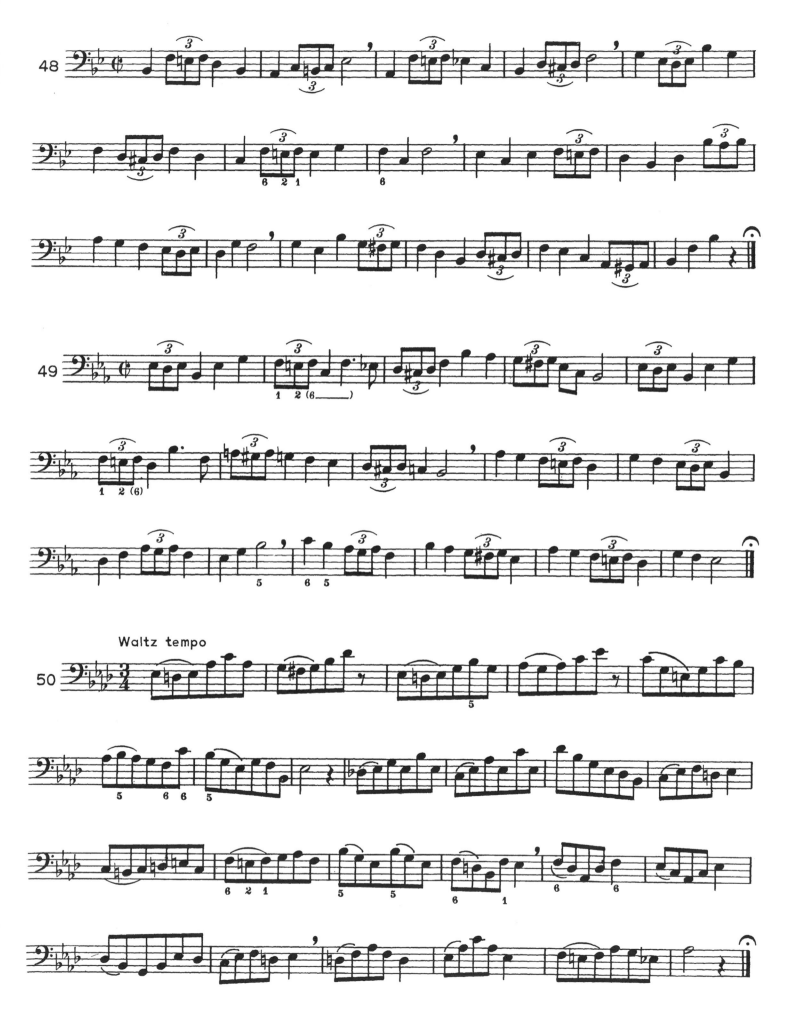

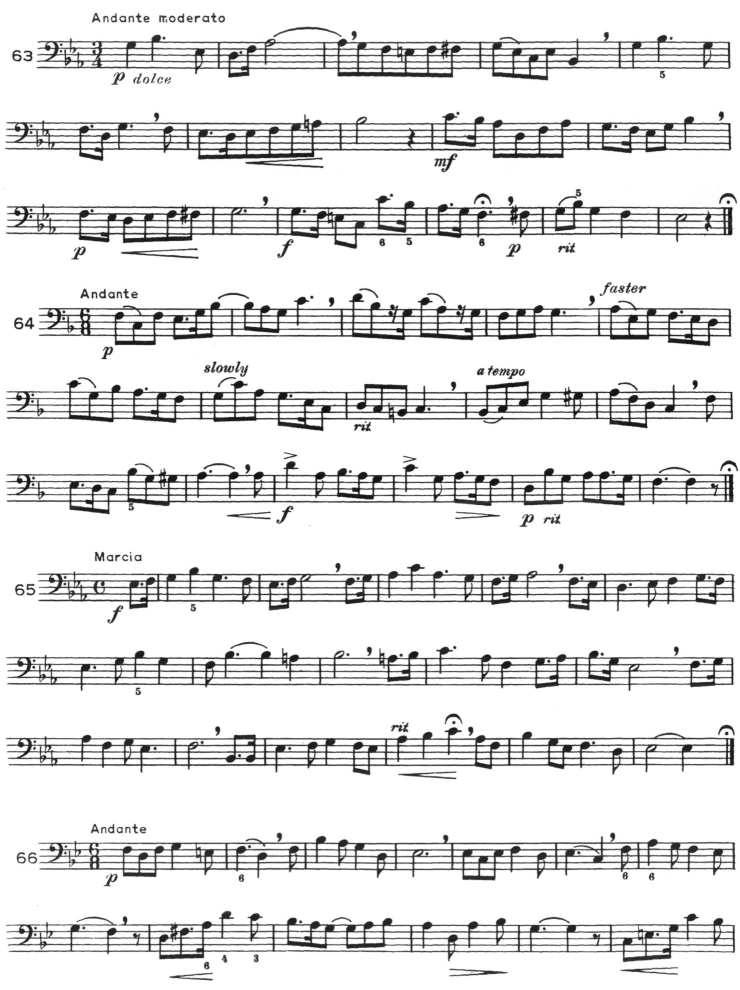

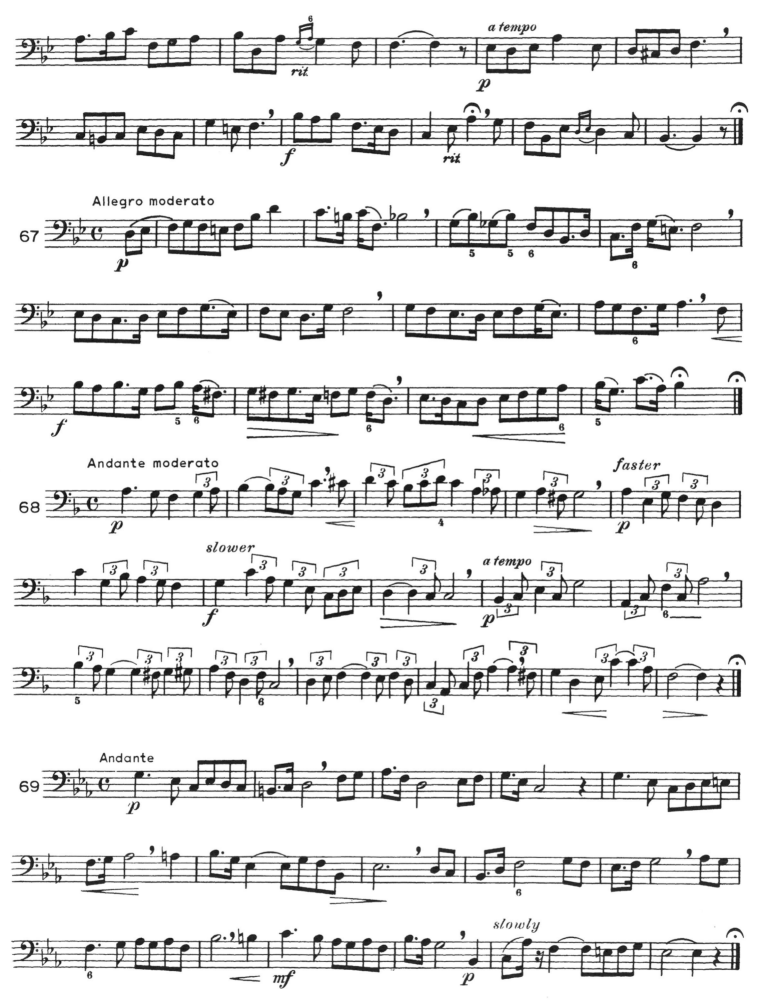

Sprightly

70

Grand March

71

Andante moderato

72

Punchinello

VANDER COOK

Debonnaire

VANDER COOK

39

Bonita
Valse Brillante

VANDER COOK